ISBN 978-1-54397-432-4

Acknowledgements

First and foremost, I pause to recognize the Almighty for giving me grace
and writing talent. I thank my wife, DeKisha, and my children,
lil' Cleophas and Jasmine, AKA "Jazzy", who have been a constant
inspiration and have endured the time and dedication it
has taken for me to prepare this reading selection.

I would like to thank <u>all</u> my family
(mom, dad, brother, sister, mommie house, gdad, gmom, Grand),
all my friends, all my co-workers, and business confidants
(Cleophas Jones Sr., Clendell Jones, G. Kelly, A. Tartt, L. Thompson, M. Williams)
who have supported me in this endeavor. I appreciate my illustrator,
Nnanna Akwu, and my colleagues, especially M. Anderson, for
helping to proofread and edit this work, and my
book consultants for publishing this book.

And following protocol, and for all those I forgot to call...Thank you.

This book is dedicated to children all over the world who are
inspired to read and *aspire* to lead...that's all children.

"UReadULead"

Follow me on Twitter at Cleophas O. Jones@ureadulead, or visit me
at www.ureadulead.com, or email me at ureadulead@aol.com

My Black History Month Project on Whoopi Goldberg starring Miss Livy

Book Summary

In this fun **UReadULead** selection, Miss Livy and the Downtown Elementary School audience proudly honor the accomplishments of Ms. Whoopi Goldberg, an extremely talented and gifted black female actress and activist. Ms. Livy conducts a live interview on stage at the school during Black History Month with Ms. Goldberg as the guest honoree. Ms. Goldberg graciously takes the opportunity to share with the school students and the audience-at-large, the commitment, dedication, determination, and work ethic it takes to become great in whatever you choose to be in life.

Enjoy reading the story and pay attention to the message Ms. Goldberg proudly shares with everyone. Is it about getting a high-quality education and being successful in life? Is it about learning to read and write proficiently? What do you think? Whatever you decide, remember – URead...ULead!!!!

Character Trait(s)
Courage and Commitment

Courage is your ability to overcome anything, no matter how hard or difficult you believe it to be. Commitment refers to how much you believe in something and how hard you are willing to work to accomplish that something. Each day in school, at home, or in the community, you demonstrate courage and commitment. Doing classwork, learning new things, making friends, following your parents' guidance, and being a good citizen, are just a few of life's experiences that require you to constantly make decisions. These decisions at times may appear to be difficult. However, your level of courage and commitment helps you to determine the best course of action to take in situations you encounter, so that you have a positive outcome.

Courage and commitment are wonderful traits to have because they help you to become a leader who can make great decisions and achieve your goals. And of course, reading is key to helping you focus your courageous and committed efforts in the right direction.

Who Are Doc Cee and Miss Livy?

Doc Cee and Miss Livy are really cool twins who share exciting adventures at home, in school, and anywhere they end up going.

Doc Cee, the elder twin, is a genius known worldwide for his advanced math and science skills. He is highly intelligent, enterprising, and athletically inclined. A natural leader, he finds himself at the forefront of situations. And he always wears his signature hat!

Miss Livy

Doc Cee

Miss Livy is the loveable, adorable twin sister who uses her wit to aid her brother and friends in their adventures. Like Doc Cee, she is academically gifted and athletically inclined. She loves reading, science, law, music, and gymnastics. Sometimes, she and her friends engage in learning adventures of their own.

My Black History Month Project
on Whoopi Goldberg

starring
Miss Livy

Written By
Dr. Cleophas Jones

Illustrated By
Nnanna Akwu

UReadULead

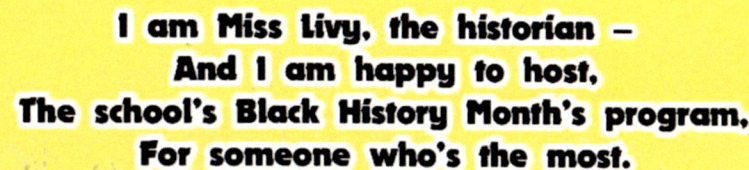

I am Miss Livy, the historian —
And I am happy to host,
The school's Black History Month's program,
For someone who's the most.

Our person to be covered today,
Is someone you might know.
But just in case by chance you don't,
Then just check out the show.

New York City, in New York —
Is where Ms. Johnson was born.
But we know her as Whoopi Goldberg,
A name that we adorn.

Manhattan's Chelsea-Elliot Houses,
Was Whoopi's childhood home.
Raised by a savvy and strong mom,
Young Whoopi learned right from wrong.

3

Let me go down the lengthy list
Of things that she has done.
Of many honors she's received —
And awards that she's won.

Two Golden Globes, an Emmy Award,
And don't forget a Grammy —
Sprinkle in a Tony Award,
And the Oscar completes this whammy.

One movie she's an actress –
She's a sassy, classy nun.
With lots of wit and wisdom,
She's an act second to none.

An actress and an activist,
She fights for what is right.
On the show that's called The View,
Her view's a pure delight.

Just to be on stage with her,
I get choked up inside.
So, if I don't stick to the script,
Please, people, let me slide.

Without delay, no further wait,
Let's bring this person out,
And let her tell her own story,
And what she's all about.

6

As Whoopi walked onto the stage,
Loud cheering filled the air.
She kindly waved to everyone,
Then, she sat in the chair.

Excitedly, Miss Livy said,
"We're glad you're here today.
You are my favorite TV host,
And I mean that, ok."

Ms. Whoopi smiled as Livy talked.
She gave a gentle grin.
"Livy, my girl, you're good at this,
But let me now chime in."

"The trophies, honors, and awards,
It's not about those things.
It's about fairness and respect,
Humanity can bring."

"It's all about the future,
And the people you will meet –
Knowledge you are charged to share,
That's truthful and concrete."

"Remember those less fortunate –
Who have nothing at all.
For you may be the one to help
Someone before they fall."

Miss Livy said, "That's really deep;
Please share more of your world –
Of how you were and what you did,
Back when you were a girl."

Ms. Whoopi paused a little bit
As she smiled at the crowd.
With children looking up at her,
She spoke and spoke out loud.

"The best of students I was not,
So sadly I must say.
But I had dreams; a good work ethic,
And I worked every day."

"When I was young, I made a choice –
And I chose my career.
I read a lot and worked a lot.
And this is why I'm here."

"My mom took me to movies,
And whenever we would go,
The place became my acting stage,
And I became the show."

"The New York Broadway plays I saw,
Helped me to learn my craft.
Acting was not an easy thing,
At times I felt the draft."

13

"I used to be a dishwasher.
Yes, that was once my job.
An honest and a humbling start,
I just say, 'Thank you Lord.' "

"But my big break did come about —
A letter I did write —
To the author of, The Color Purple,
My career rose like a kite."

"In many movies I have starred,
And comedy I've done too.
I've had my share of ups and downs,
But always, I came through."

"Make no mistake, the risk I took,
When choosing my career.
But if I couldn't read or write,
No doubt, I'd not be here."

"I'd like to take this time to say,
And listen with both ears —
Read and write and study your math;
You read, you lead, you hear?"

Miss Livy stood and clapped her hands.
The audience clapped as well,
Miss Livy said, "You're something else."
The crowd let out a yell.

16

"You know, Ms. Whoopi, you're some showgirl;
You are an awesome big timer."
Ms. Whoopi replied, "A showgirl I'm not;
What I am is a classic headliner."

Thank You!!
Ms. Whoopi Goldberg

Miss Livy said, "True that. True that.
And I'm delighted to say,
That for this year's Black History Month,
We proudly recognize you today!"

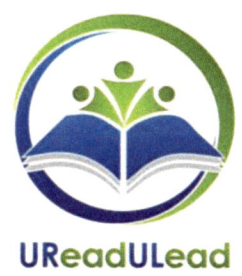

UReadULead

Standards Based
College and Career Readiness

This UReadULead literary selection contains Dolch sight words and incorporates the following English Language Arts Reading Standards:

- Actively engage in group reading activities with purpose and understanding of characters, main idea, setting, plot, conflict, and resolution
- Synthesize and deduce (determine) the meaning of the story from illustrations and supporting details
- Analyze and explain how words and phrases in the story or poem suggest feeling and appeal to the senses
- Interpret, compare and contrast illustrations and details in a story to describe its characters, setting or events
- Identify and explain how words and literary terms in the reading selection supply rhythm and meaning in a story, poem, or song
- Determine the meaning of words and phrases as they are used in a text, distinguishing literal from nonliteral language
- Provide exposure to challenging vocabulary words and synthesize the meaning of the words based on their usage in the text

This literary work is aligned with the following Social Studies Standards:

- Explore and explain similarities and differences in the ways groups, societies, and cultures address similar human needs and concerns
- Analyze a particular event to identify and expound upon reasons individuals might respond to it in different ways

Standards derived from common core standards, www.corestandards.org

UReadULead Favorites

Buy these favorite books and more at, www.ureadulead.com

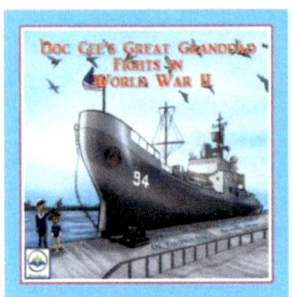

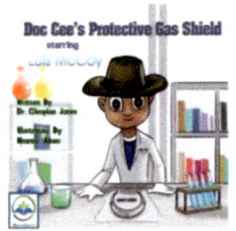

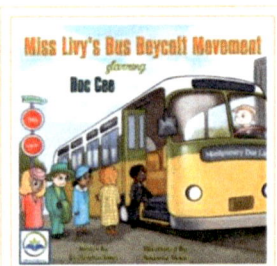

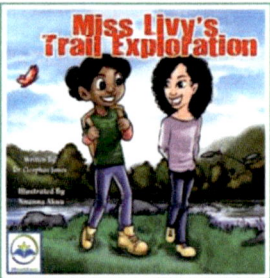

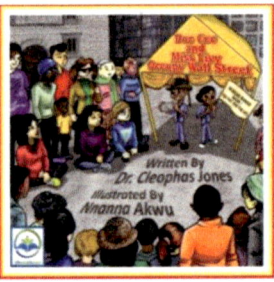

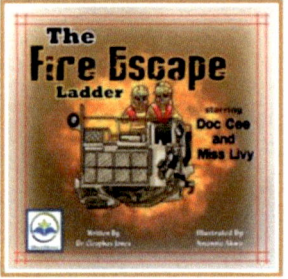
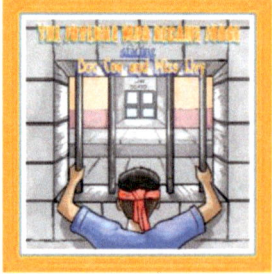

UReadULead

FUN-TIVITY: <u>Expository Essay Writing Made Easy</u>

An expository essay is one of the four types of major essays. The purpose of an expository essay is to state the facts. Below is an example of an expository essay about Mr. Henry T. Sampson.

Have you ever heard of Dr. Henry T. Sampson? Do you know what he invented? Well, neither did I until I did some research on who discovered the cell phone. The facts about this invention are astonishing as you will learn from the writing.

Do You Know Who Really Invented the Cell Phone?

Henry T. Sampson was born in Jackson, Mississippi, in 1934. This young black male scholar would grow up to become nothing short of a genius and one of the greatest inventors in the field of engineering. In fact, without his invention, the world would not have one the most useful and needed communication devices that we rely so heavily upon today – the cell phone. Henry T. Sampson graduated from Lanier High School in Jackson, Mississippi in 1951. He attended Morehouse College for two years and then he transferred to Purdue University where he graduated with a Bachelor of Science degree in chemical engineering in 1956. In 1961, he graduated from the University of California in Los Angeles with a Master's Degree in engineering. He continued his graduate college studies at the University of Illinois at Urbana-Champaign, and in 1967, he became the first black man in the United States to earn a Doctorate of Philosophy (Ph.D.) in nuclear engineering. On July 6, 1971, Dr. Sampson was awarded a patent, with George H. Miley, for the creation of a gamma-electrical cell device that produces a high voltage electricity from radiation sources. Dr. Sampson's brilliant invention makes portable cell phone communication possible, all by using radio waves to transmit and receive audio signals. Without his invention, cell phone communication may not exist today.

Website Reference: http://greaterdiversity.com/meet-henry-t-sampson-man-created-first-cell-phone-back-1971/

Fun-Tivity: In the space below, you are to write your own expository essay about a famous inventor, scientist, athlete, doctor, soldier, or anyone you choose. The essay must contain at least four sentences. Watch your grammar and spelling, and remember to use the facts to help you create your sentences. Feel free to use the above expository essay as a guide.

| |
| |
| |
| |
| |
| |
| |
| |

TO MY READER – THANK YOU!!!!!!!!

Hello to you, my reader;
I'm writing just to say,
That hopefully this awesome book
Has helped to make your day.

The fun and rhyming literature
Is purposeful indeed;
It's meant to help its audience
To learn and to succeed.

And so I'll leave you with these words
So magical to me,
That if you read, then you will lead –
Successful you will be.

UReadULead